CODING

1

2

3

JANET SLINGERLAND

starting with STEAM

Rourke
Educational Media

rourkeeducationalmedia.com

Before & After Reading Activities

Teaching Focus:

Consonant Blends—Look in the book to find words that begin with a consonant blend such as st, sm, or pr.

Before Reading:

Building Academic Vocabulary and Background Knowledge

Before reading a book, it is important to set the stage for your child or student by using pre-reading strategies. This will help them develop their vocabulary, increase their reading comprehension, and make connections across the curriculum.

1. *Read the title and look at the cover. Let's make predictions about what this book will be about.*
2. *Take a picture walk by talking about the pictures/photographs in the book. Implant the vocabulary as you take the picture walk. Be sure to talk about the text features such as headings, Table of Contents, glossary, bolded words, captions, charts/ diagrams, or Index.*
3. Have students read the first page of text with you then have students read the remaining text.
4. *Strategy Talk – use to assist students while reading.*
   - *Get your mouth ready*
   - *Look at the picture*
   - *Think…does it make sense*
   - *Think…does it look right*
   - *Think…does it sound right*
   - *Chunk it – by looking for a part you know*
5. *Read it again.*

After Reading:

Comprehension and Extension Activity

After reading the book, work on the following questions with your child or students in order to check their level of reading comprehension and content mastery.

1. *Describe how coders code.* (Summarize)
2. *What does a coder do when they find a bug?* (Asking Questions)
3. *What is an algorithm?* (Asking Questions)
4. *Have you ever used a computer? If so, what have you used it for?* (Text to Self Connection)

Extension Activity

Pick a common everyday activity like brushing teeth, washing hands, or eating breakfast. Write an algorithm for this activity. Break it down into simple steps. Write out the steps. Make sure the steps are in the proper order.

Table of Contents

Rourke
Educational Media
rourkeeducationalmedia.com

Computers

Computers are **machines**. They **solve** problems. They make things work.

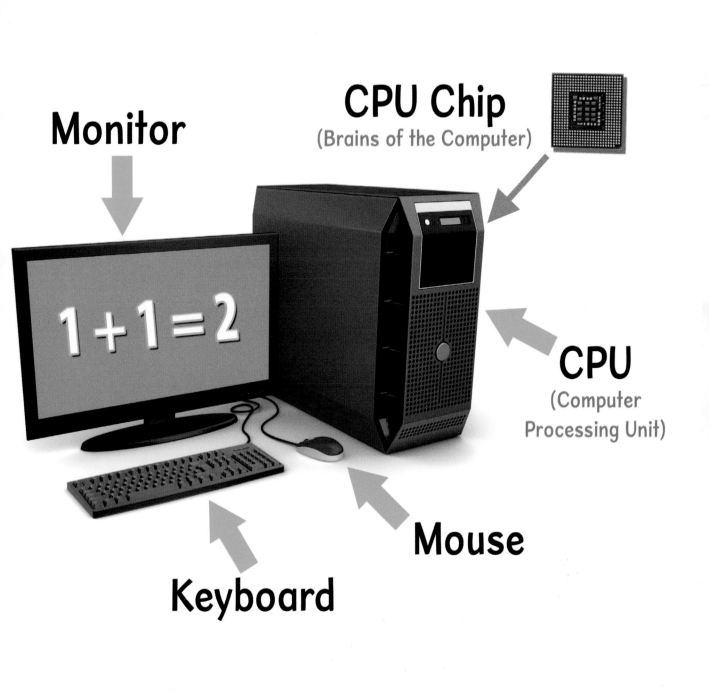

Monitor

CPU Chip
(Brains of the Computer)

$1 + 1 = 2$

CPU
(Computer
Processing Unit)

Mouse

Keyboard

Computers are in big things. They are in small things. Cars have computers. Some watches do too.

A smartwatch is a wearable computer.

Coders

How does the computer know what to do?

Code! Code is a set of **commands.**

A binary code uses the digits 0 and 1 to give the computer instructions.

Each computer uses different commands. A coder is a person who writes code.

Writing Code

Step 1

A coder writes an **algorithm**. This is a set of **steps**. It tells how to do a job.

STEP ONE — Fetch toothbrush

STEP TWO — Fetch toothpaste

STEP THREE — Put toothpaste on toothbrush

STEP FOUR — Put toothbrush in mouth

STEP FIVE — Brush your teeth

STEP SIX — Rinse and spit

A coder turns the steps into commands. They use commands the computer knows.

Code:

```
<1DOCTYPE html>
<html>
<body>

<h1 style="color:blue;">Hello World</h1>
<p style="color:red;">Welcome. This is a paragraph.</p>

</body>
</html>
```

Result:

Hello World

Welcome. This is a paragraph.

The coder runs the code. There is a **bug**. Not a real bug! A coding bug is a mistake.

The coder fixes the bug. They run the code again. Are there any more bugs? No. The code works!

Coders must test code over and over until there are no more bugs.

Maker Activity:

Code an Escape

You will need:

- ✓ 1-inch (2.54 centimeter) square graph paper
- ✓ coin or button
- ✓ pen or pencil

- Create a maze using the lines of the graph paper.

- Mark the start and end of the maze.

- Write arrow steps. Show how to move the coin or button through the maze.

→ move one block right

← move one block left

↑ move one block up

↓ move one block down

This is code.

Give the maze and code to a friend.

Have them follow the commands.

Can they move the piece through the maze?

Photo Glossary

algorithm (AL-geh-rih-them): A set of steps used to solve a problem or accomplish a goal.

bug (BUHG): A mistake in a machine.

commands (kuh-MANDZ): Orders that have to be followed.

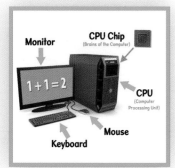

machines (mah-SHEENZ): Pieces of equipment that use power to make or do something.

solve (SAWLV): To find an answer to a problem.

steps (STEHPZ): The small actions that make up a big job.

Index

Meet The Author!
www.meetREMauthors.com

Further Reading

Kelly, James Floyd, *The Story of Coding*, DK, 2017.

Lyons, Heather, and Elizabeth Tweedale, *A World of Programming*
    (Kids Get Coding), Lerner, 2017.

Wallmark, Laurie, *Grace Hopper: Queen of Computer Code*,
    Sterling Children's Books, 2017.

About the Author

Before writing books for children, Janet Slingerland wrote code. She spent 15 years programming computers in things like submarines, telephones, and airplanes. Janet lives in New Jersey with her husband, three children, and a dog.

www.rourkeeducationalmedia.com

PHOTO CREDITS: Cover, Title Page & Pg 3 ©ratselmeister, Pgs 4, 6, 8, 10, 12, 14, 16, 18, ©iunewind, Pg 11 & 22 ©mediaphotos, Pg 17, 22 ©fizkes, Pg 5 & 23 ©adempercem, Pg 7 ©Prykhodov, Pg 8 ©frender, Pg 9 ©kaptnali, Pg 19 ©courtneyk, Pg 21 ©ulimi

Edited by: Keli Sipperley
Cover and Interior design by: Kathy Walsh

Library of Congress PCN Data

Coding 1, 2, 3 / Janet Slingerland
(Starting with STEAM)
978-1-64156-422-9 ISBN (hard cover)(alk. paper)
978-1-64156-548-6 ISBN (soft cover)
978-1-64156-670-4 ISBN (e-Book)

Library of Congress Control Number:
Printed in the United States of America, North Mankato, Minnesota